It's the Little Things

"Don't be afraid to make a bold entry statement that reflects who you are," says Jeannette Whitson. In her own home, via ferns and foliage—both living and created—she sends a marvelous message that, "gardens have no boundaries here."
DESIGNER: JEANNETTE WHITSON

FOLLOWING PAGES
In his Manhattan master bedroom (painted in varying shades of his favorite blue) textile designer John Robshaw uses an antique campaign chest from India to display beloved objects from his constant travels, including a headdress from Zimbabwe.
DESIGNER: JOHN ROBSHAW

Thom Filicia's lake retreat reflects his mantra for
collected, casual, and personalized living, and
where tablescapes reveal accumulated treasures
and the memories that come with them.
DESIGNER: THOM FILICIA

Every table—no matter how grand—
deserves some flights of fancy.
DESIGNER: TIMOTHY CORRIGAN

22

U.S. POSTAGE
WINCHESTER, TENN.
MAR 2
5 30 PM
1917
Mr. George Kopmeier
1434 Cherokee Rd
Louisville, Ky.

In every cluster of details, there should always be an element of surprise. Otherwise your eye doesn't stay involved.
DESIGNER: **GEORGE KRAUTH**

The textures of materials play a starring role when
it comes to creating landscapes that capture the eye:
matte and gloss, smooth and rough delight the eye
in elegant juxtaposition.
DESIGNER: HUBERT ZANDBERG

Faux bamboo, American folk art, decorative Asian —
ethnic treasures add a hit of luxury that doesn't take
itself too seriously: "They're all the design elements
I believe in," says designer Betsy Burnham.
DESIGNER: BETSY BURNHAM

It's all about layering, both in height and textures: a floral pattern is the ideal backdrop for a framed portrait that stylishly serves as a focal point. The glass touches in the front stay low and deftly pick up the blues-y color scheme.
DESIGNER: JACQUELINE COUMANS

Designer Charlotte Moss understands that by displaying beloved treasures in a thoughtful, well-edited manner, we give our most treasured objects the opportunity to inspire us on a daily basis.

DESIGNER: CHARLOTTE MOSS

When arranging, more is more,
especially when each varies in size
and texture. It should never feel fussy,
but rather, artfully accumulated.
DESIGNER: STEVEN JOHANKNECHT

35

When a budget dictates creativity, the result can still feel just as luxe. "Many of my clients' rooms must serve dual purposes," says designer Kishani Perera. This interesting metal credenza hides her printer, files, and other office elements. With the tablescape arranged on top, it turns into a conversation piece for her dinner guests.

DESIGNER: KISHANI PERERA

A somber bureau plays beautifully with both
lighthearted and sacred details. A mix of moods
always creates the most dynamic visual landscapes.
DESIGNER: SIG BERGAMIN

A room's exotic mood — here, in Morocco — is created when like-minded objects correlate without being too in sync.
DESIGNER: MERYANNE LOUM-MARTIN

40

"A framed collage found in Paris sets the tone for this vignette in my home," says David Scott. "The group of accessories pulls from architectural forms inspired by the art, and the contrast of dark and light, shiny and matte, leads to a comfortable tension. I believe that all good things go together."
DESIGNER: **DAVID SCOTT**

"In my Manhattan apartment I like to mix old and new with a touch of color and a little bit of fun," says Rebecca de Ravenel. "My favorite things are the collage my father had painted for me, the Claude Lalanne lamp my godfather gave me, and the giant green bottle I bought in Maine that was sent to the Bahamas and then made it unscathed from there to New York. It's the little things that have a history, the details, the patterns, and, of course, some pretty flowers that make any room come alive!"
DESIGNER: REBECCA DE RAVENEL

In the New York screening room of designer Howard
Slatkin, details are integral in creating a mood that's equal
parts fantasy and familiar. That's because Slatkin infuses
everything with a deeply personal touch: the French
orientalist picture sits atop Indian printed cotton panels
that Slatkin dipped in tubs of tea. Shells he has collected
since childhood fill a French Régence-mounted Chinese
Ming-period jardinière as well as a pair of marble tazza.
DESIGNER: HOWARD SLATKIN

Objects look so much grander when they aren't displayed in too serious a manner. Whimsy and confidence are décor's best friend.

DESIGNER: MICHAEL EICKE

FOLLOWING PAGES
Gold and vintage accents (not to mention faux crocodile paneling) give a feminine edge to a sitting area that feels as glamorous as it does inviting.

DESIGNER: DEE HUTTON

48

A bedside table is an everyday staple with the potential to feel one of a kind. Why not use ornamentation to elevate the functional to the fantastical?
DESIGNER: KATIE RIDDER

THE GARDEN TOURIST*
ROSENFELD

TWOMBLY NURSERY   Spring 1998-1999

Taylor's Guides Perennials
BARBARA W. ELLIS

Living Jewels

Flowers of Silk and Gold   MERRELL
                                                    THE TEXTILE MUSEUM

Scandinavian Design   HEATHER SMITH MacISAAC

PEPERONN

ATHOME   SUZANNE RHEINSTEIN   R

MARIMEKKO   FABRICS
                                            FASHION
                                            ARCHITECTURE   BGC YALE

ALEXA HAMPTON   *The Language of Interior Design*

WALLPAPER

A room's details can be both charming and practical: Here, a built-in daybed with flanking shelves not only maximizes storage but really gives its young occupant a special place to display all of her favorite things. The cameo pillows of her very own silhouette further personalize the space and are the perfect finishing touch.
DESIGNER: MELISSA WARNER ROTHBLUM

The details of the very things that help display our
things can be as interesting as the things themselves.
Here, in Jonathan Adler and Simon Doonan's Shelter
Island home, different textures of wood offer further
dimension and character to a bookcase's treasures.
DESIGNER: JONATHAN ADLER

56

Compatible colors and textures can unify
disparate objects just enough so that the
eye can enjoy them either in one fell swoop
or linger and admire each individually.

In India Hicks's home in the Bahamas, the
sea's bounty is displayed with a formality that
elegantly contrasts with the casual collection of
inspirational images gathered below. The effect
feels deeply curated and deeply personal.
DESIGNER: INDIA HICKS

Painting the inside of a cupboard an unexpected
color, like verdant green, gives the pieces it displays
a surge of fresh energy and slightly exotic powers.
DESIGNER: AGNES EMERY

62

An all-white kitchen is just the backdrop to display
accents of wood: the combination feels both rustic
and ethereal. "With its boundaries stripped," says
its owner, photographer and stylist Kara Rosenlund,
"fine art can be displayed in this hardworking space."
DESIGNER: KARA ROSENLUND

It's the Little Things

CREATING BIG MOMENTS IN YOUR HOME THROUGH THE STYLISH SMALL STUFF

SUSANNA SALK

RIZZOLI
NEW YORK

New York · Paris · London · Milan

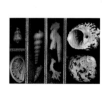

CONTENTS

Introduction

It was in a spectacular setting in December in the Connecticut countryside: a holiday party being celebrated in a grand room made mostly of glass. More greenhouse than party space, it was filled with giant lemon trees instead of furniture and white gravel instead of carpets. Classical music wafted through the air like a warm summer wind belying the snow drifts outside. Champagne was being passed and guests were eagerly making their way to greet the hostess, whom I hadn't yet had the pleasure of meeting, having scored an invitation through my friendship with her daughter. Instead I escaped to the kitchen for a minute. It's a game I like to play: Can I meet the owner by meeting the house first?

In my own home, it's the combination and juxtaposition of meaningful details that bring emotion to every room and make me happy every time I see them. It's all about making the everyday feel less ordinary.

In her quiet kitchen the unfolding details were like speedy brushstrokes painting a revealing self-portrait: a dusty yet complete spice rack; art by young grandchildren sharing space with water-colored landscapes. A row of orchids along a windowsill interspersed with sea shells clearly found on a beach not bought in a store; an invitation to a benefit for a local land trust organization; an NPR bag holding library books on Cleopatra and Woody Guthrie. Lemons in a bowl straight off a potter's wheel, fashioned by eager yet beginner hands. Her purple silk scarf was draped over a chair, forgotten in haste to greet company. It was all here: a life, past, present,

TOP LEFT

Details should feel edited to have the greatest impact and the only pedigree they need is personal meaning. This chest I found online starts to feel more exotic when it's paired with a flea-market lamp I scored with my best friend in tow, a photograph I surprised my husband with on our anniversary, and a prop stick I procured from one of my favorite shoots.

BOTTOM LEFT AND OPPOSITE

Whether on my entry hall table or guest bedroom, I try enliven the smallest spaces with splashes of color or pattern, either man-made or nature-made. Details not only bring depth and life to a room, they remind our guests they are visiting a home, not a hotel.

and future, told through the daily details, more eloquent than words, more vivid than photographs. I could pick my host out of a crowd anywhere in less than a minute.

Details aren't about just having stuff around in your house or putting a lamp on an end table and calling it a day. When chosen with care, they can create lush landscapes, where the eye delights in both the macro and the micro. The individual moments are enhanced through juxtaposition with one another. It's not necessarily through commonality, but by the chemistry of the combination and happenstance.

Rooms come alive through their details: whether their arrangement be deliberately curated or casually cramped, the constant is always editing with an eye towards the beloved, the curious, the deeply personal.

I try to use furniture as a stage upon which all the details, like actors, then play upon. I never take the opportunity too seriously, yet I make sure every moment and accessory counts. Whether swapping out a beige lampshade for racy red, or investing in the most beautiful fireplace screen I can afford, the little moments become the biggest.

Inside the rooms you're about to meet (because we meet rooms as much as people) you'll be able to delight in what delights others in every area of the house: whether hung along walls, gathered around a kitchen sink, strung across a fireplace mantel, or arranged across tabletops, it's the little things that count.

Details can be luxurious, like the embroidered velvet backs of curtains that play delightful peekaboo or walls layered in sumptuous papers of fearless pattern. Or practical: hardware as elegant as jewelry, soft pillows as interesting as the company they help coddle. Details can form a quiet still life from nature brought inside to live in a quiet nook, or they can be spotlighted via a man-made collection showcased front and center for all to admire.

I wanted to create a book that gathered all these great moments and celebrated them under one roof, so to speak, because we can't be lucky enough to be invited everywhere. *It's the Little Things* is my way of introducing you to the hundreds of interesting lives and memories that are hosted through detail without ever leaving your armchair.

Because when it comes to decorating, I have come to realize it's not God in the detail . . . but the very essence of human nature itself.

Surfaces

Across your coffee table, around your kitchen sink, above your
wet bar, or on your kitchen shelf: every surface in every area of
your home is waiting for you to create a visual landscape that
delights yet doesn't feel overly staged. When done correctly,
these moments keep you not only inspired on a daily basis but,
through their thoughtful order, centered. Use only things you
love and love to look at. There should be power in the form of
the object, no matter if it's a sponge dish, an alarm clock, or a
precious vase. Consider every surface's possibility and know that
deciding to keep it bare is as important a decorating decision as
anything you could ever purchase.

How do you create a definitive mood without it looking too thematic? By ensuring that there's harmony in the details without too much similarity. A pop of pink ensures the somber tartans and florals don't take themselves too seriously.

DESIGNERS: WARD DENTON and CHRISTOPHER GARDNER

14

"The color green is a very big factor in our décor," says Ted Kennedy Watson, of the Seattle abode he shares with his husband Ted Sive. "Not only in paint color, but in objects. We find many of the things on our travels, which is one of my very favorite ways to collect. Grouped together all the 'things' tell a happy visual story."
DESIGNER: **TED KENNEDY WATSON**

67

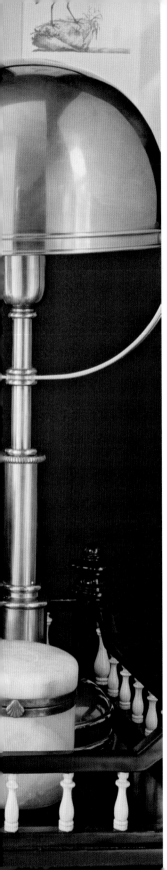

The idea of a drink may lure you in, but it's the details
that make you want to linger longer and explore: fresh
flowers, a jaunty brass lamp, tiny paintings exquisitely
framed, all make the very most of the moment.

69

When is a bar so much more than a bar? When its base is as exotic as the potential drinks that may be poured, when presentation counts as much as content and pieces with a past are cherished.
DESIGNER: ERICA TANOV

70

This small bar, which was once a closet in a home office, has become a modern-day cabinet of curiosities, showcasing its owners' prized travel treasures and family heirlooms. The vibrant aubergine and white pear block-print Indian fabric on the walls serves as the most elegantly exotic of backdrops.

DESIGNER: ELLE CLYMER AND STEPHANIE WOODMANSEE
OF HENRY & CO DESIGN

"The mirror and glass nook in this kitchen was a perfect opportunity to display curated treasures, barware, and a moment of glitz," says Chicago designer Summer Thornton. "It's the different layers that make this little moment so interesting: each shelf accessorized a little bit differently, things intentionally mismatched – those details helped inject personality and character and keep the eye moving."

DESIGNER: **SUMMER THORNTON**

A bar should never be just a place to fix yourself a drink. It should feel like its own little destination, apart from the rest of the home, while still reflecting the owner's distinct character through its details.
DESIGNER: CHARLES JAMES

Imagine your wall is a giant frame waiting to be filled with color, texture, and visual life. Whether you cover it with a striped wallpaper that makes your heart race, a shade of yellow you crave, or an oil portrait of somebody else's ancestor you found at a flea market, walls should reflect the details of our inner passions and outer lives. So use them wisely yet don't take them too seriously. Without personality, a white wall reminds us it is merely there to shelter us. Infused with detail, it becomes as vital to a room's décor as its furniture.

The easiest way to enliven an entryway is via detail. Here, Alessandra Branca injects a jolt of warm red that's the ultimate backdrop for an assemblage of accessories to pop against.
DESIGNER: ALESSANDRA BRANCA FOR ELLE DECOR

A 1960s pool house gets transformed into a
country retreat for a lucky guest via textures like a
rope headboard, limed-oak armchairs upholstered
in cowhide, and pine walls washed in white.
DESIGNERS: BRUCE GLICKMAN and WILSON HENLEY

An unexpected color can beautifully set off a room's objects, so choose one that can be impactful without being overwhelming. A turquoise blue is a hue you never tire of admiring.

DESIGNER: CINDY SHERMAN

FOLLOWING PAGES

The gilded candelabras, the graphic wallpaper from Sweden, and a custom-upholstered headboard are the classic structural details that hold designer Gary Spain's room together. "These bold elements, along with the symmetry, allow for my naturally whimsical and eclectic taste to work without it looking too insane," says Spain.

DESIGNER: GARY SPAIN

Beds shouldn't just be comfortable, they should make
every effort to express your style spirit: from creating a
headboard that has the rich formality of a dining room
chair to monograms that are anything but monotonous,
the doing is in the details.

DESIGNER: ALESSANDRA BRANCA FOR ELLE DECOR

How to make a pair of twin beds not feel too juvenile?
Dress them up with bold black and white details—
from bedding to plates floating like dreams above—
that aren't too serious.
DESIGNER: BIBI MONNAHAN

"Powder rooms provide a unique opportunity to indulge in
a bold gesture or two," says designer Tommy Smythe. "You're
here for a good time, not a long time, so a bold wall treatment
or color scheme is appropriate in a way they may not be
in a dining room or a bedroom. I also like to ensure that
where pedestal sinks are employed, a small table be added
somewhere to provide a surface. A lady will inevitably visit
with her handbag and I'm guessing she won't be enthused
about putting it on the floor."
DESIGNER: TOMMY SMYTHE

"We always think of small powder rooms as little jewel boxes where we can use explosive color," says the design team of Tilton Fenwick. They practice what they preach by coating every square inch of this diminutive space with dazzling wallpaper.
DESIGNER: TILTON FENWICK

95

A little breakfast nook off of a kitchen gets a big dose
of personality from New Orleans-based designer
Melissa Rufty. A medley of patterned wallpaper and
fabric is grounded by a rustic altar table.
DESIGNER: **MELISSA RUFTY**

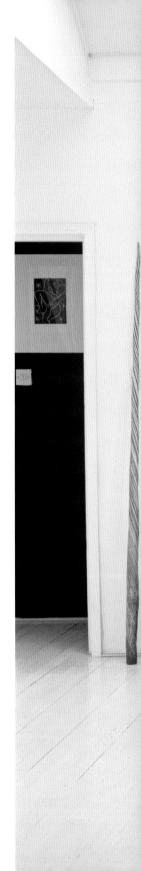

Paint a room and floor white, choose white for its main furnishings so that they seem to disappear . . . then let the details do all the talking.

Often nostalgia proves the mother of invention, or rather, reinvention. Designer Tom Scheerer developed the bamboo Chippendale wallpaper based on a green on white version he grew up with in his family's East Hampton sunroom in the sixties. The pattern is a rich layer behind a Victorian dressing table refashioned as a vanity. The Brancusi-esque stool gives a modern snap.

DESIGNER: TOM SCHEERER

Masculine details such as the dark chocolate brown
walls, white subway tiles, and vintage photos of soldiers
gallantly anchor the whimsical capiz-shell chandelier.
DESIGNER: **GARY SPAIN**

FOLLOWING PAGES
A kitchen's details needn't be only practical: a dash
of whimsy not only spices up its standard proportions
but makes any chore seem far less ordinary.
DESIGNER: **ASHLEY WHITTAKER**

102

Color punctuates like nothing else.
Here, varying shades of green enhance
a room's art and architecture.
DESIGNER: RICHARD HOLLEY

Designer Alex Papachristidis—here in his
own home—relies on details like pattern and
texture to create lush depth and visual delight.
DESIGNER: ALEX PAPACHRISTIDIS

The very presence of books in a room doesn't merely reflect an owner's intelligence but an avid curiosity of all that remains outside its walls. The room, as a result, doesn't just feel contained with knowledge, but passion as well.

DESIGNER: J. MORGAN PUETT

111

For designer Howard Slatkin
it's all about the rich mix of
details—from both exotic
and local destinations—in his
Manhattan bedroom. Atop
the rare Louis XVI mahogany
tables by master woodworker
Canabas, are fifties lamps with
Bakelite shades. The Louis XVI
canapé is covered in emerald
silk velvet that Slatkin had
hand-quilted in a geometric
pattern. The small wicker table
is from Target.
DESIGNER: **HOWARD SLATKIN**

113

Katie Ridder understands how to balance the elements while still creating bits of surprise along the way so your eye is never bored. Here, a thoughtful wall arrangement is given an extra jolt thanks to a whimsical lampshade, an unexpected stack of books beneath the table, and a lively rug pattern.

DESIGNER: KATIE RIDDER

114

In designer Lorenzo Castillo's own Madrid home,
the graphic rug is a modern counterpart to the
old world layering of the room's rich details. It
cohabitates happily alongside the other colors and
textures while at the same time challenging them.
DESIGNER: **LORENZO CASTILLO AND THE RUG COMPANY**

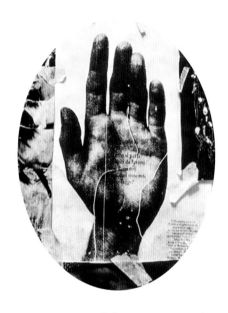

A kitchen nook becomes as much a
hub for artistic creativity as it does
for culinary concoctions, thanks to
Ann Shore's collage of inspiring
black-and-white-images. Even the
refrigerator becomes a canvas.
DESIGNER: **ANN SHORE**

118

When it comes to displaying what you love, beauty (not to mention floors and paint) may fade with time but never diminish. So only worry about the details that count: cherished art, sharing a drink with friends, and furniture with history.

DESIGNERS: DUNCAN GRANT AND VANESSA BELL

Repeating a detail—especially across
a wall—creates harmony and allows a
variety of proportions to coexist below.
DESIGNER: AMANDA LINDROTH

Groupings of accessories can be hung in artistic clusters to bring
detail and character to a lonely wall. Here, variations on a black
tray feel as much like an installation as a treasured collection.
DESIGNER: **JOAN OSOFSKY**

FOLLOWING PAGES
White isn't the only wall color upon which art shines. Black
is just the hue to display Federico de Vera's moody mix of
nineteenth-century European portraits and contemporary
paintings. It feels both modern and antiquated all at once,
and therefore timeless.
DESIGNER: **FEDERICO DE VERA**

124

Elevate the everyday by arranging simple
china into a chic cluster on a wall. The black
and white patterns—punctuated by the all-
white plates—pop against the dark wall. It's
an easy and inexpensive way to turn a blank
slate into a stylish one.

DESIGNER: GREG NATALE

"I began with one vintage snapshot, years ago, an image of young men hanging out at a sidewalk café, smoking cigarettes and wearing spiffy outfits," says filmmaker and photo stylist Jeffrey Moss. "It sparked in me a fever of collecting. I then amassed so many photographs that it was impractical to frame them all and so I began pinning them directly to the wall, in a sort of grid that I fancied was reminiscent of the warp and woof of fabric. Eventually it became an all-out frenzy of controlled chaos."
DESIGNER: JEFFREY MOSS

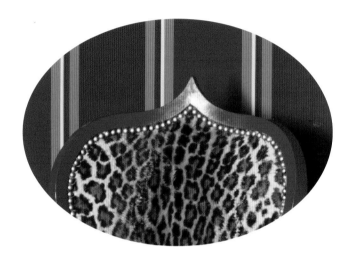

Mixing rich patterns—such as stripes with leopard—
turns them into livable neutrals, especially paired with
luscious artwork. You don't need to have a chateau to
re-create this look: all it takes is the confidence to go
bold at home.
DESIGNER: GÉRARD TREMOLET

FOLLOWING PAGES
Designer Alex Papachristidis layers bold patterns and
exotic accents—ranging from the custom to the flea
market find—throughout his own living room with
both a masterful and fanciful hand.
DESIGNER: ALEX PAPACHRISTIDIS

Mantels

A bare mantel is like a woman's unadorned neck. As beautiful as its natural surface is, it calls out to be draped in a thoughtful yet playful way that enhances the beauty of its owner. Don't just throw a pair of ordinary candlesticks on its surface and call it a day. Why not cluster a collection of candles in different heights and textures instead? Or conversely, try many of the same. More is more as long as it's edited. The key is not in the monetary value but in the emotion behind the arrangement. A mantel accessorized well beckons us closer, like moths to a flame.

When Meredith Kurosko created her stationery
company Regas, she wanted the hearth in the studio
to be a physical reflection of the Regas team's warm
approach to the creative process. It was through
the process of collecting visual details to adorn the
fireplace that she realized the assembled mix was
telling the story of her personal journey toward
becoming a business owner.
DESIGNER: REGAS

Nº 28865

Why should a fireplace be just for fires? It can also be a
cornerstone to many accessories, which can seemingly
float above, around, and even below its architecture.
Bits of nature further the fairy tale feeling.

Miles Redd composes rooms the way F. Scott Fitzgerald
composed sentences: with a dash of wit, punctuating
color, lyrical romance, and glamour with just a bit of edge.
DESIGNER: **MILES REDD**

142

Don't waste the opportunity a fireplace mantel gives you
to create a well-edited, lyrical moment full of varying
yet balanced heights. Gold finishes are just the right
glamorous touch amongst the wood and natural elements.
DESIGNER: **CARL PALASOTA**

144

Combining varying hues of like-minded colors can
create an artful landscape. Bricks with an indigo palette
offer just enough moody contrast for the collection
of blue and white below. The coral cuts down on the
formal factor with its elegantly earthy vibe.
DESIGNER: JASON BELL

146

Here in his own chateau in France,
Timothy Corrigan proves that chateau
living is magical instead of fussy when
whimsical details are displayed on surfaces
usually reserved for formal arrangements.
DESIGNER: TIMOTHY CORRIGAN

Creating a room that resonates with the senses requires
a rich layering of details from ceiling to floor. Start with a
"wow" lighting fixture and surround it with pieces that are
of equal depth and character.

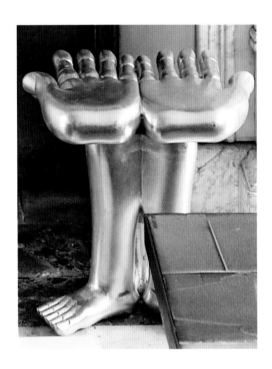

Clutter can be chic when it's curated. Art
and anthropology from every walk of life
find a common bond when displayed in
such an intimate manner, floor to ceiling,
in a Paris apartment.

DESIGNER: SACHA WALCKHOFF

152

It's not only the content of the
collected objects that makes a surface
well composed. The play of scale—
rough with smooth, matte with
metallic, and hard with soft—lends
itself to visual excitement and balance.
Try placing a single static object next
to a series of frenetic ones.
DESIGNER: FAWN GALLI

"Accessories are the finishing touches that make a room feel interesting and complete," says designer Timothy Corrigan, who practices what he preaches most eloquently here in his own home in France. "Mixing pieces from different periods and places provides the contrast that lets you appreciate them each individually and as a grouping. Most of all, don't take it so seriously!"
DESIGNER: TIMOTHY CORRIGAN

Upholstering a living room's walls, curtains, and sofa
in stamped crimson velvet not only enriches a large
space, but gives it a fantasy element. It also provides
a lush backdrop for a stunning art collection.
DESIGNERS: ANN GETTY AND THOMAS BRITT

Little Moments

Think of the little details in your room like punctuation marks in a sentence: when misused, the room reads as overcrowded and rushed with no place to pause. However, when used effectively, details make a room feel almost lyrical. It's all about making your mark: Why buy curtain tie backs from the hardware store when vintage ones plucked from a yard sale make your curtains look that much more interesting? Why line your books on a white shelf when you could stack them against a color that sets off their titles? The more thought and time you give to creating the little moments, the more they will ultimately inspire in big ways.

"Layers matter," says Texas-based designer Denise McGaha. "Custom navy-and-violet-skirted bedside tables are amped up by the addition of chartreuse back-painted-glass tabletops. These tables—along with a timeless geode sculpture—make for a tableau not soon to be forgotten."

DESIGNER: DENISE McGAHA

162

STYLE AND SUBSTANCE

ELLEDECOR STYLE AND SUBSTANCE

PHOEBE HOWARD The Joy of Decorating

PRIVATE VIEWS

Owners John Knott and John Fondas knew the secret to transforming this former hotel in Maine into their beloved summer retreat was to energize its room with detail, both in the blue and white patterns they love and an American style that feels both nautical and exotic.

DESIGNERS: JOHN KNOTT AND JOHN FONDAS

Objects don't need to always
remain perched on top of a
shelf: floating them just above or
below the surface gives a magical
effect and extends the power of
the landscape.

In a kitchen, fluttering butterflies show
that no matter how small, when placed just
right whimsy can have a big visual impact.
DESIGNER: PIERO FORNASETTI

Why not echo a whimsical detail from your rug pattern both
in the classical lines of furniture and its modern color?
DESIGNER: DIAMOND BARATTA

FOLLOWING PAGES
Details shouldn't just be there to decorate and cover a space.
They are a tactile reminder of a life well lived: beloved
journeys, stories savored, and favorite memories captured.
DESIGNER: JILL SHARP BRINSON

Our goal was to add objects that felt like they were collected over time," says Chris Barrett. "This Italian vintage mirror had the kind of patina we were looking for above the bedside table. Old and new combined always makes for an interesting juxtaposition."
DESIGNER: CHRIS BARRETT

Lavishing details on curtains—these featuring custom
hand-embroidered cuffs on silk—adds a couture element
to an everyday design staple, like cuff links to a shirt.
DESIGNER: CULLMAN & KRAVIS

176

Hardware is an ideal way to express
your inner fancy—not to mention
humor. It's an inexpensive and
instant way to transform existing
pieces and provide another visual
layer to a room.
DESIGNER: AMY FINN BERNIER

Thanks to designer Katie Ridder's artful eye, a bedside
lamp becomes as pleasing as it is illuminating.
DESIGNER: **KATIE RIDDER**

The key detail can often be enhanced due to the impact
of pattern: an antique Chinese chair is revived with the
addition of a snappy box pillow in a timeless Chiang Mai
Dragon pattern from Schumacher.
DESIGNER: **DENISE McGAHA**

Harmony is struck by landscapes not being too balanced:
a cluster of three blue bottles is more interesting than one
of each at either end. The rich turquoise, sea green, and
deep browns of the oil painting ground the arrangement,
which is then reflected in the accompanying objects.
DESIGNER: **KARA ROSENLUND**

182

In John Derian's apartment, the practical behind the creative—such as wires and switches—take on an artistic flair when displayed with equal confidence.
DESIGNER: JOHN DERIAN

Big Moments

A room full of big moments is only as big as the integrity of its littlest. A wall covered with a collection of trays will look cluttered if the space's three other walls haven't been culled with equal thought. A sofa's unique upholstery trim will go unnoticed if the surfaces of the coffee and end tables around it feel scattered. That chandelier's big personality will be diminished if the table below it has no star power. Not every piece everywhere has to have a big ego but they all must have a raison d'être. No matter how varied the elements, if their common denominator is your passion for them they will all cohesively coexist.

"I always find design to be a balanced mixture of nouns and adjectives," says Scot Meacham Wood. "The nouns (chair, lamp, carpet) are about working with proportion and scale, with a clear eye on function. The details are the adjectives (pattern, detail trim, texture) and where the real fun takes place. In this little view of my own entryway, we're simply playing with adjectives.
DESIGNER: SCOT MEACHAM WOOD

No need to be so corporate when it comes to your workspace. Tom Scheerer's is the perfect example of how an office's many details can fuel creativity instead of clutter.
DESIGNER: TOM SCHEERER

FOLLOWING PAGES
A special piece of furniture deserves to be surrounded by equally unique details: from the walls to the art to the doorframe's detail, everything here echoes the exotic yet cozy vibe of the black bookcase. As a result, the room's many elements relate to one another like lively dinner conversation among friends.
DESIGNER: GÉRARD TREMOLET

You can tell so much about someone—their dreams and their daily lives—just by the details found in their entry hall.

DESIGNER: REGINE LAVERGE-SCHADE

194

Whether coming or going, make the most out of your entry by having fun with each of its surfaces. Graphic black and white allows many different patterns to play in one space with its unifying two hues.

DESIGNER: MARYAM MONTAGUE

"When it came to designing my own home in Nantucket, my husband and I decided to experiment with a 'pure white box' inspired by a trip to Denmark," says designer Gary McBournie. "But we had also just been to Marrakech and I needed a bit of pattern and some color. So I decided to paint the floor with large orange and white squares on the diagonal, which also helped to expand the space. Much to my delight, when I opened the back door I was treated to the wonderful interplay of the marine blue against the orange of the floor."

DESIGNER: GARY McBOURNIE

There's no detail more crucial to setting a room's tone than a rug. Here, both comfort and quirky coziness play an integral part thanks to a pattern that offers a rustic feeling with a modern twist. "Tartan is usually very traditional, but when woven on the diagonal and with vibrant colors, it injects modernity to a hunting lodge," says Suzanne Sharp, cofounder and creative director of The Rug Company.

They say a leopard never changes its spots, so designer Melissa Rufty gave this stair runner a little shot of contrasting hot pink trim. "Little custom details," says Rufty, "are sure to give your guests something to really talk about."
DESIGNER: MELISSA RUFTY

Pets are the ultimate elements that make a room feel
truly complete, no matter how stunning its décor.
They reflect not just our passion for domesticity but
our ability to share the spaces we love.
DESIGNER: WILLIAM WALDRON

This proves that bathrooms have the
potential to be magical spaces. After
painting the walls an unexpected color, it's
then all about bringing in formal elements
from other rooms in the house and taking
the focus away from the utilitarian stuff.
DESIGNER: CORNELIA BAYLEY

The social center of the Williams Rosselli household,
this massive room in the property's barn becomes a cozy
spot for gatherings, thanks to its generously proportioned
furniture and abundance of accessories, thoughtfully
arranged from floor to ceiling. Every available space is
occupied with something to either delight the eye or make
guests feel right at home.
DESIGNER: BUNNY WILLIAMS

Everything looks heightened against a colored
backdrop. A dark hue on a wall feels both luxe and
dramatic and makes all the surrounding details—
no matter how casual—that much the richer.
DESIGNER: OLIVIER GAGNÈRE

Old world meets new and has a fantastic time when dashes
of color are woven into the mix, both to punctuate and unify.
DESIGNER: GERT VOORJANS

It's amazing how much wonderful detail can thrive in a single corner if we take the time to consider the top-to-bottom possibilities: from fanciful floor tiles, lush wall coverings, and orderly frames hung unconventionally, the dreamy cohesion comes from the like-minded color hues.
DESIGNER: PIERO CASTELLINI

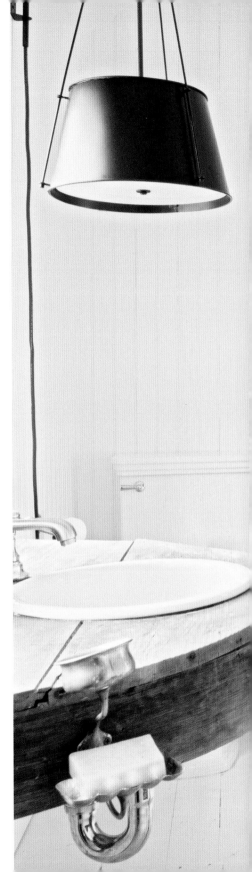

In designer Darryl Carter's Virginia retreat, a pre–
Civil War cottage shows that the details of what has
been taken out are as important as what has ultimately
been put in. "I removed all the embellishments from
the previous owners and took the room back to its core
in the spirit of its deep history," says Carter. "The tub is
reclaimed and I put the hunt scene above as an homage
to the bucolic setting and animals at play around me."
DESIGNER: DARRYL CARTER

216

Using elegant yet unexpected details and materials, like
a nineteenth-century French iron-and-marble sink,
oval-backed French chairs, and vintage iron scrollwork
sconces, designer Bunny Williams transforms a humble
guest bathroom into a space that has the friendly
formality of a dining room.
DESIGNER: BUNNY WILLIAMS

218

From its very threshold a house's soul can
be brought to life through details. Here,
variations on black and white set a lively
yet refined tone.
DESIGNER: HILLARY THOMAS

"Glamour is the keynote in this space used
for cocktails before dinner with guests," says
designer Gideon Mendelson. "Lush turquoise
velvet banquettes are set in all four corners to
create a lively hubbub throughout the room.
The gold of the lamps and silk pillows, like
good jewelry, provide accents, while a large
center mirror adds to the festivities since
people tend to be more animated when they
can see themselves reflected."
DESIGNER: GIDEON MENDELSON

FOLLOWING PAGES
The open living space of this loft comprised
of several seating areas (a dining room, the
kitchen, and the blue-lacquered library)
dictated that each be distinguished by dozens
of details, which are evenly—yet never
expectedly—woven throughout. "We kept the
walls neutral and used the colors as accent
until you get into the library, where you are
surprised by this pop of color," say the design
team of Tilton Fenwick. "The library is the
room that ties everything together."
DESIGNER: TILTON FENWICK

222

Adding dramatic details between rooms can heighten
the view from one room to the next: here, lush curtains
are equally fetching from either direction.
DESIGNER: RICHARD HOLLEY

FOLLOWING PAGES
A little pattern goes a long way in this vibrant den.
"Enough is never enough," says Melissa Rufty, its
designer. "Just when you think the room is complete,
pile it on. The end result is layered and rich."
DESIGNER: MELISSA RUFTY

The impact of shapes in a space cannot be overstated: here, the grounding grid of windowpanes is the ideal counterpoint to the curves in the nearby furniture. The absence of a carpet allows the forms to really look their sensuous best.

DESIGNER: DANA HARPER

Reminders are everywhere that this is an island house in
Maine with both a unique history and location. Not to mention
delightful details that never take themselves too seriously.
DESIGNERS: JOHN KNOTT AND JOHN FONDAS

233

"A kitchen should reflect your personal style as much as any room in the home, and for me this means lots of femininity, elegance, and a little dash of the unexpected," says Christine Dovey. "When creating this dining vignette, Meredith and I focused on lighting, and finding the perfect vintage fixtures was a really important detail to the overall look. I was thrilled to find this pair of pink Murano beauties in a local shop."
DESIGNERS: MEREDITH HERON DESIGN and CHRISTINE DOVEY STYLE

FOLLOWING PAGES
Kitchens come alive through detail, and not just in hardware. Here a gutsy lighting fixture—not to mention red dinosaur— brings instant whimsy to a space so often treated too seriously. The sophisticated artwork nicely balances out the levity.
DESIGNER: OLIVIER GAGNÈRE

234

Gary Spain likes to call this room "Mad
chaos in sync. Parisian ateliers, Yves Saint
Laurent, and color inspired me. The classic
lines and familiarity of the furniture and
the gilt frames create the base and then you
layer in the details of fun from there."
DESIGNER: GARY SPAIN

238

Details can bring so much life. Combining
personal artwork with warm textures such as
rattan and wood against lots of white and then
adding a splash of feminine color suddenly makes
an ordinary corner feel as personal as a bedroom.
DESIGNER: INDIA HICKS

240

So often we're afraid to have too much detail in a bedroom: we believe it has to be pared down otherwise it won't feel restful. But this room feels lush and cocoon-like despite its rich palette. Lively patterns are kept to the floor so as not to be too distracting and, as a result, the bold colors almost feel like neutrals.

DESIGNER: BIBI MONNAHAN

FOLLOWING PAGES

In his seaside retreat in Provincetown, Ken Fulk brings to life a guest room with nostalgic details that make the space not only reflect its nautical and historical surroundings, but also feel timeless. The number on the door gives each visitor their very own assigned destination.

DESIGNER: KEN FULK

"The funny thing here is that nothing in this room is intentional," says designer Tommy Smythe of this bedroom he once lived in. "The table is the one that fit best and it just happened to be of the same era and wood species as the bed. The raffia-covered ottoman beneath the table was simply added to provide an extra surface for the many magazines and books I like to have close at hand, giving relief and needed real estate to the tabletop above. The buffalo plaid coverlet, lamp base, ball fringe, and oval mirrors work as a team here. I call them 'blackcents.'"

DESIGNER: **TOMMY SMYTHE**

246

Packing a lot of color and detail into
a space like a bedroom requires the
balance of pairs so that the mood stays
serene without being too somnolent.
DESIGNER: HUBERT ZANDBERG

248

This small bedroom—an addition to a one-hundred-year-old restored cabin in Jackson, Wyoming—is brought to life with crisp details and materials culled locally and from around the globe. Beds upholstered in Belgian linen look even chicer when draped with Pendleton blankets.
DESIGNER: CARNEY LOGAN BURKE ARCHITECTS, LINDA PERLMAN INTERIOR

This bedroom designed by
Alessandra Branca is the
stylish sum of its many parts.
From the zebra rug on the
floor to the acid green walls
enveloped in her own damask
linen for Schumacher, Branca
creates a jewel box effect by
mixing time periods and rich
textures, top to bottom.
DESIGNER: ALESSANDRA BRANCA
FOR ELLE DECOR

253

To help a small space morph from the functional to the inviting, unique details were brought in: a set of antique doors painted black and then hung on a ceiling track, their frosted glass etched with the words "laundry room." A floating shelf above a butcher-block counter provides a display surface for artwork and pretty accessories.

DESIGNER: CHRISTINE DOVEY STYLE

"I worry little about how things go together," says Jeannette Whitson of her home. "For me it is always about a visual balance of scale, texture, tone, and form. Decorating and cooking have always seemed so similar to me finding the balance in visual and taste, I rely not on rules and recipes but on an organic alchemy of disparate things."
DESIGNER: JEANNETTE WHITSON

256

"My design style has been tremendously influenced by the books that I have loved," says Lisa Borgnes Giramonti. In her Los Angeles foyer, she papered the walls in Clarence House's "Flowering Quince" because she wanted visitors to feel like they were walking into her own secret garden. The life-size sheep is a reminder of the ones dotting the landscapes of all her favorite nineteenth-century novels, with the Dutch door lending a "Middlemarch" charm to urban living.
DESIGNER: LISA BORGNES GIRAMONTI

Details always make the larger picture dense and more exciting, creating a delicious depth that is clever, tender, and unique. Here, the embroidered Greek key trim on the taffeta drapes; a vintage gilded wheat-sheaf sconce; a gem-studded sunburst mirror, the incredible mural with a jib door (complete with black doorknob); and a coverlet made from a washed canvas drop cloth then hand-painted, do just that.
DESIGNER: VALORIE HART

FOLLOWING PAGES
Little things feel big when their abundance helps tell the story of whoever is behind their proud display. Here, whimsy and balance do a delightful tango, never letting one overwhelm the deft moves of the other.
DESIGNER: PODGE BUNE

DESIGNER CREDITS

PHOTOGRAPHER CREDITS

Front cover: Tria Giovan
Back cover: Charlie Maier

4: Thayer Allyson Gowdy

6–11: All photos by Carol Dronsfield except
lower bedroom photo on page 8, which is
by Constance Schiano

SURFACES

14: Vincent Knapp / The Interior Archive

16: Jeannette Whitson, Garden Variety Design

17–18: William Waldron

21: Eric Piasecki

23: Alexandre Bailhache

24: Tria Giovan

27: Simon Upton / The Interior Archive

29: Lisa Romerein

31: Simon Upton / The Interior Archive

33: Edward Addeo

34: Simon Upton / The Interior Archive

37: Jean Randazzo

39: Simon Upton / The Interior Archive

41: Richard Powers

43: Antoine Bootz, from *Outside the Box* /
Pointed Leaf Press

45: Josh Gaddy

47: Tria Giovan

49: Tria Giovan

50–51: Carol Dronsfield

53: Eric Piasecki

55: David Fenton

57: Richard Powers

58, 59: Mary Rozzi

60: Michel Arnaud / The Interior Archive

63: Richard Powers

65: Kara Rosenlund

66: Ted Kennedy Watson

68: Mary Rozzi

71: Richard Powers

73: Victor Harshbarger

75: © Miki Duisterhof —
www.mikiduisterhof.com

76: Tria Giovan

WALLS

80: Douglas Friedman

83: William Waldron

85: Tria Giovan

BIG MOMENTS

ACKNOWLEDGMENTS

I'd like to profusely thank all the designers who contributed to this book: You continue to wow me with your passion for life's little moments and the joy they can bring. And your generosity knows no bounds.

And to every photographer here who so aptly translated these details into big moments with your unique lens: Thank you!

I'm also so grateful for my beyond-talented team at Rizzoli who continues to believe in me: My beloved editor Ellen Nidy (who embraces the stylish small stuff as easily as she breathes) and Rizzoli's fearless leader, Charles Miers. And Jason Snyder: way to rock the book's design!

First published in the United States of America in 2016 by
Rizzoli International Publications, Inc.
300 Park Avenue South, New York, NY 10010
www.rizzoliusa.com

Book design by Jason Snyder
Rizzoli Editor: Ellen Nidy

2021 2022 / 10 9 8 7 6 5

ISBN-13: 978-0-8478-4807-2
Library of Congress Control Number: 2015956953

Printed and bound in China

Distributed to the U.S. trade by Random House